How to Remember Not to Forget

How to Remember Not to Forget

By Joan Who? and Adam Rosensomething

Written by Joan Houlihan
and
Adam Rosenbaum

iUniverse, Inc.
New York Lincoln Shanghai

How to Remember Not to Forget
By Joan Who? and Adam Rosensomething

iUniverse, Inc.

For information address:
iUniverse, Inc.
2021 Pine Lake Road, Suite 100
Lincoln, NE 68512
www.iuniverse.com

ISBN: 0-595-32946-2

Printed in the United States of America

Contents

Preface

Memory on Everyone's Mind

Memory is a subject on the collective minds of our aging population. Go to any bookstore or magazine stand and you'll find the topics of memory and Alzheimer's disease featured prominently. As we're exposed increasingly to this information, we consider our own memory function, as well as the mental health of our loved ones. Questions and concerns arise as to whether our memories are working properly and whether an imperfect performance indicates the onset of Alzheimer's.

How to Remember Not to Forget by Joan Who? and Adam Rosensomething provides answers and guidance to many of these questions and concerns, as well as a time-tested system for memory improvement that was born out of personal struggles with memory.

You will discover a unique combination of theory and practical advice that's easy to understand and requires little effort to apply; you will learn quickly how the memory process works, why it fails, and how you can fix it.

The Story Behind the System

In 1986, Joan Houlihan was a part-time teacher and a full-time mother of four boys and one girl, living in Westfield, New Jersey. Her life was full and fun with soccer, cub scouts, dancing lessons, piano, religious education, and a home-based eyeglass business. But in February of that year, the unexpected happened.

Joan's husband Peter was diagnosed with malignant melanoma and died four months later. With her oldest child in college and the youngest still in grammar school, Joan took a full-time job as an administrator in a local hospital to make ends meet.

Unfortunately, her life as a working single mother was overwhelming and complicated. She was under tremendous stress, couldn't concentrate, and was having bouts of mild depression. Inevitably, Joan realized her memory wasn't working properly, and with so many responsibilities, she needed a solution.

She began to keep a notebook of ideas and strategies for memory improvement to help her remember not to forget. Over the years, as her collection of notes grew, she discovered that she had documented a simple system of practical solutions to help just about anyone with common, everyday memory problems.

Additionally, as her career began to evolve, her time and attention were drawn increasingly to the needs and frustrations of those who suffered from memory loss. Joan began to incorporate her memory system into the programs she designed for residents in the facilities she managed. She called her system "Memorology."

Having proven the success of Memorology, Joan decided it was time to share her discoveries with others, so she contacted her friend and former Westfield neighbor, Adam Rosenbaum.

Adam, who is the same age as Joan's third son Patrick, grew up in the neighborhood and was affectionately thought of as the Houlihan's sixth adopted child. After graduating from Rutgers University in 1993 with a degree in Physics, Adam landed a job as a computer analyst at a pharmaceutical company in Madison, New Jersey. In this position, he traveled frequently to South America and Europe to install accounting software and train workers on the systems.

Adam's career gradually progressed into new roles as a software training consultant and project manager. Like Joan, his interest in memory was piqued by his work, which in his case centered on the practical application of adult learning methodologies at all levels of the corporate hierarchy—from the workers on the factory floor to the senior managers.

As he traveled around the world, both for work, and whenever he could as a backpacking tourist, Adam kept travel journals, which he edited into short stories that he sent to family and friends, including Joan. His narratives of time spent "walking the Earth," in combination with the knowledge of adult education and instructional design he had garnered in his profession, were the reasons Joan decided to team up with Adam to introduce Memorology.

Although they are separated in age by nearly thirty years and are positioned at much different stages in their careers,

Joan and Adam share a common imagination and positive spirit, and you will discover their optimism in this book.

The Authors

Joan Houlihan is the Executive Director of Atria Woodbriar Assisted Living in Falmouth, Massachusetts. This community is home to over one hundred residents who suffer from difficulties with memory, including Short-Term Memory loss, dementia, and Alzheimer's disease. Joan speaks frequently on Cape Cod and in the Boston Metropolitan area on the topic of memory and senior healthcare. She also teaches a "mini-university" for aging adults at Atria Woodbriar, exploring the frustrations and fears surrounding memory loss. Joan has degrees in Education from Boston College and Boston University. She lives in East Sandwich, Massachusetts.

Adam Rosenbaum is a software training consultant who develops training programs for private companies and government agencies. He specializes in instruction for SAP accounting and manufacturing software in North and South America, and he has applied a number of methodologies used in adult learning in creating this book. Adam is completing a Masters degree in Instructional and Performance Technology at Boise State University. He lives in Davis, California.

1.

Introduction

Memorology is a new field of research that studies how powerful forces of interference known as Memory Busters can muddle up your mind and lead to varying degrees of brain blockage and a condition of absentmindedness known as "the memory lapse." The Memory Busters are:

- Information overload
- Inattention due to lack of interest, confidence, or motivation
- Mindless repetition
- Unhealthy habits
- Stress
- Depression

This Memorology manual shows you how to achieve a high-performance memory and how to avoid those frequent flashes of forgetfulness by learning to control the impact of the Memory Busters before they have a chance to turn your brain into lukewarm porridge.

To help you realize this goal, we recommend the following course of action as you delve into the details of the pages ahead and beyond:

1. Tell yourself your memory is already rock-solid. You may have convinced yourself otherwise, but hold on. You're only on the first page of this book.
2. Read *How to Remember Not to Forget by Joan Who? and Adam Rosensomething* cover-to-cover.
3. Keep a copy close by and refer to it on a regular basis.
4. Practice what you learn.
5. Most importantly, when you put this book down, remember where you left it!

Now get ready for a new reality inside the realm of Memorology.

2.

Memorology 101

I Remember It Well

Have you ever had one of those days when you forget to pick up the dry cleaning, lose your glasses, miss a dentist appointment, and cannot remember the number of your Cousin Lucy who lives in Reno, even though you phone her five times a week?

Do you frequently forget simple things like where you parked your car at the grocery store or the names of the new neighbors you met fifteen minutes ago?

Have you started to suspect that your memory is on a different vector in the space-time continuum than the rest of the population, and you're just a few years away from having cotton balls for brains?

As experienced Memorologists, we want you to know you have nothing to fear; your memory can be as sharp and efficient today as it was twenty years ago.

In the following pages we've combined more than a decade's worth of research, interviews, and careful observations to help you discover how your memory works and explain why sometimes it seems like it's running out of gas. Most importantly, we offer a treasure chest of tools to help you get your memory back on track, even on those days when your brain is half asleep, long after your second cup of coffee.

As you make your way through these chapters, you'll realize that remembering not to forget is easy and enjoyable. Once you put your Memorology knowledge to work, the results will be visible immediately, though you'll feel like you're making no effort at all.

The Good News

The good news about memory is that just about anyone who forgets can learn to remember not to forget. Dates, words, numbers, names, and belongings are misplaced and forgotten more because of the Memory Busters than anything to do with memory loss.

Regardless of your age or the color of your hair, you can start along a path to an improved memory by taking the first step in Memorology; recognize that you do not have a "bad memory," because nothing is wrong with it.

Instead, start to think about your memory in terms of efficiency. Once you look at it from this point of view, improvement won't seem like such a far-fetched idea; it's easy to identify and eliminate the forces that interfere with your good memory, causing it to become inefficient.

To demonstrate further the importance of efficiency in memory improvement, let's first have a look at how your memory works and describe what it's made of.

3.

What is Memory Anyway?

Three Types of Memory

Human memory is actually a process of three independent components that work together simultaneously:

1.   Sensory Memory
2.   Short-Term Memory
3.   Long-Term Memory

Sensory Memory

The memory process begins with Sensory Memory, which is like a sponge that picks up and holds onto everything you see, hear, feel, taste, and touch, but only for about one second. In this short period of time, your brain works to analyze and prioritize a tremendous amount of information in order to filter out details that aren't important.

This means that if a sight, sound, or smell doesn't happen to grab your *attention*, your brain has decided the particulars aren't worth the time or the effort, and the sensory information disappears from your mind faster than you can say "lickety split."

Here's an example of Sensory Memory in action: Mr. Jones is watching a football game on TV while his wife Gertrude sits next to him and talks to her friend Trudy on the phone. We know that Mr. Jones hears the entire conversation, but he's not paying attention to it, and he won't be able to remember anything his wife says since the chat with Trudy is just a lot of background noise that goes in one ear and right out the other.

But what happens if the scenario changes and Gertrude suddenly says to Trudy, "Oh! You know? My husband told me you could find one of those gizmos at the Home Depot!"

Well, now Mr. Jones' ears are going to perk up because hearing his name and "Home Depot" in the same sentence catches his attention, and just like that, his brain sends this new noteworthy information over to the next stage of the memory process: Short-Term Memory.

Short-Term Memory

When Short-Term Memory receives sensory information, it stores the data for about thirty seconds, so Mr. Jones will take a few moments to decide whether the words he's heard about Home Depot are *meaningful* or *relevant*.

If the information is not meaningful or if it cannot be related to other memories already recorded in his brain, it will be forgotten. On the other hand, if it is meaningful or relevant, or if it can be *rehearsed*, the information stands a good chance of being encoded into Mr. Jones' Long-Term Memory.

Here's an example of how Short-Term Memory works in combination with Sensory Memory. Say that Trudy wants to know the number of Home Depot so she can call to ask if they're carrying the aforementioned gizmo. Unfortunately, Trudy doesn't have a phonebook because she used up the pages to line the cage of her pet parakeet, Percival.

As a favor for Trudy, Mrs. Jones walks over to her kitchen where she keeps the Yellow Pages, but she doesn't want to schlep the heavy phonebook all the way back to the TV room. Instead, after finding the number, she repeats the digits out loud over and over again as she returns to the phone.

Mrs. Jones realizes the phone number is nothing more than a random list of figures that have no inherent meaning. By rehearsing, she uses sound to repeatedly refresh her Short-Term Memory and foil an escape of the information before the timer in her brain reaches thirty seconds.

As soon as she picks up the receiver, she relays the information to Trudy, and the mission is accomplished without any heavy lifting.

For years, Madison Avenue has also known how Short-Term Memory functions, and they've spent millions of dollars creating clever commercials that make their products more meaningful and memorable by working with the memory process.

For example, Dial-A-Mattress of New York doesn't ask you to call them at 1-800-628-8737, because the number means nothing and they know you'll never remember it. Instead, they tell you, "Dial 1-800-MATTRESS."

Now you remember the company, the product, and you know how to reach them because their entire message is associated with the letters on the telephone that spell the product they're selling, which they happen to repeat over and over again.

The company has made their telephone number so meaningful to your Short-Term Memory that your brain encodes it into your Long-Term Memory, which you'll be able to retrieve for years to come.

Now, who are you going to call when you want to buy a mattress?

Short-Term Memory Exercise

To see an example of how your Short-Term Memory works, give this fifteen-second exercise a try. Don't turn the page until you've read this short list of instructions:

1. Find someone who can time you for fifteen seconds, or get a kitchen timer.
2. Grab a pen and a piece of paper.
3. When you read the word *GO!* at the bottom of these instructions, turn the page and study the list of words for fifteen seconds.
4. When fifteen seconds are up, turn the page.
5. *GO!*

Strawberry

Bed

Soccer

Baseball

Hockey

California
Apple

Cherry

Maine

Chair

Pennsylvania   Dresser

Sofa

Basketball

Football

Michigan

Table

Alabama

Orange

Texas

Peach

Banana

Desk

Wrestling

Now take thirty seconds and write down every word you can remember. Don't peek!

How many items did you remember? If you are like most people, out of the twenty-four words listed, you probably wrote down between five and nine. This is a typical result that demonstrates the storage limitations of Short-Term Memory when information is presented in an arbitrary and scattered way.

However, your Short-Term Memory will operate more efficiently when information is "chunked" together into neatly organized categories. For example, which set of numbers is easier to remember?

1 7 7 6 2 0 0 4 1 9 4 1

or

1776   2004   1941

Here's another question: Do you think you would have remembered more words if they had been chunked this way?

Sports	Fruit	US States	Furniture
Soccer	Strawberry	Michigan	Bed
Football	Orange	Alabama	Sofa
Hockey	Banana	Pennsylvania	Dresser
Wrestling	Cherry	Maine	Chair
Baseball	Apple	California	Table
Basketball	Peach	Texas	Desk

Probably so, but we didn't give you a chance to analyze the patterns. Since the world doesn't present information to you in neat packages, we spread the words all over the page to imitate reality. In the chapters ahead, one of the ways you'll learn to improve your Short-Term and Long-Term Memory is to chunk the information in your life together. You'll see that it's a very effective way to beat the Memory Busters.

Long-Term Memory

Your Long-Term Memory contains encoded information that is either meaningful or so well-rehearsed it may never depart from your mind. Since there are no time limits to Long-Term Memories, Mr. Jones may not ask his wife whether Trudy made it to Home Depot until later that day, or even the following week. It's even possible that ten years later he might ask Mrs. Jones, "Do you remember that time when you were talking to Trudy, and she needed to know where I bought those gizmos?"

This is the same reason why you can retrieve meaningful personal experiences from your Long-Term Memory—a first date, a first kiss, an unbelievable embarrassment—"like it was yesterday."

Long-Term Memory can sneak up on you out of nowhere. Imagine visiting a city for the first time in thirty years. As you walk down a familiar street, you look around and recognize a restaurant where your father bought you a vanilla ice cream cone three decades ago. You hadn't thought about that afternoon for years, but now you remember what the weather was like that day, the expression on the face of your waiter, even the color of the clothes you were wearing.

Incredibly, the brain can hold onto a lifetime of Long-Term Memories, even when Short-Term Memory has failed.

Adam's grandfather Ely suffered true memory loss, resulting from Alzheimer's disease. Towards the end of his life he didn't even know what decade he was living in. Yet he could tell you stories from when he was a twelve-year-old boy selling peanuts in Sportsman's Park in St. Louis during Cardinals baseball games.

His greatest baseball memories came from the 1926 World Series when he watched the Cardinals take on Babe Ruth, Lou Gehrig, and the Yankees. Even with Alzheimer's, he could still recount how St. Louis won in New York when Ruth was tagged out trying to steal second base in the bottom of the ninth inning of game seven, and how he ran out onto the streets to sell a special edition of the St. Louis Post Dispatch, earning enough money to support himself and his mother for a month.

He was just a young boy at the time, yet those images from seven decades ago were still clear in his memory. And just like listening to Ely's stories, it is fascinating to watch how an old-time sing-along can maintain the interest and participation of the residents of a dementia wing in a nursing home. Why? When the group starts singing these songs from the 1930s and 40s, they remember every word.

The Memory Process

The illustration below outlines the memory process and shows the relationships between Sensory, Short-Term, and Long-Term Memory.

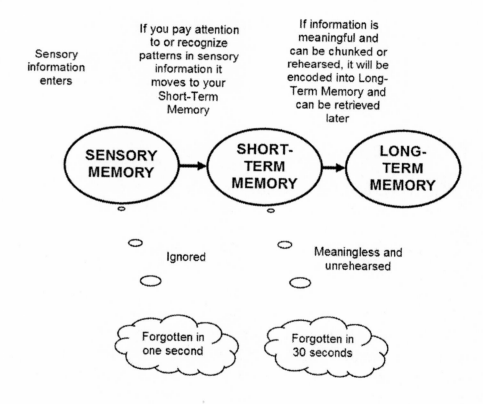

4.

The Memory Busters

Why We Forget

You've learned that memory is really a process that blends sensory, short-term, and long-term components into a highly coordinated operation. And you've also discovered that attention, meaning, and rehearsal are the super-octane gasoline that keeps this engine running.

So with all of this new information, the logical question to ask is, "How can I apply what I know to improve my memory?"

Well, as we mentioned earlier, the first step in Memorology is to recognize that you have a wonderful brain, with all of the working parts and all of the power you'll ever need in order to have an extremely efficient, high-performance memory.

Secondly, realize that your inability to recall facts, figures, dates, and your Cousin Lucy's phone number in Reno is most often a symptom of the Memory Busters—six invisible clouds of interference that prevent you from paying attention, associating meaning, and chunking the important information you want to remember. Again, they are:

- Information overload
- Inattention due to lack of interest, confidence, or motivation
- Mindless repetition
- Unhealthy habits
- Stress
- Depression

When these lightning bolts strike, your memory's performance is as dependable as a leaky roof on a rainy day, and no one can escape them, including the authors of this book. Take a look at some examples of how inattention, information overload, stress, and mindless repetition have affected the lives of Joan and Adam.

Have You Ever Had Days Like These?

Joan Houlihan:

Bored, tuned out, and shut off. There are some things I'm just not interested in, like hooking up a VCR.

My son Tim always shows me how to hook up the television to our broken VCR. He says, "Now if I'm not here, just pull this cord, loosen this thingamajig, and screw this doodad in like so. It's simple."

So Tim goes out one Friday night, and later my sister comes in with two videos. Guess what? I'm in Massachusetts calling my son John, who's still at work in Los Angeles.

"Hello, is John there?"

"I'm sorry, he's in a meeting. Who's calling please?"

"It's just his mom."

"Hold on. We always stop meetings for moms."

"No, no! I just need directions on how to hook up my VCR!"

The voice on the other end couldn't stop laughing. "Excuse me, John, it's your mother. She can't get the VCR to work."

Aahhh!!!!

Adam Rosenbaum:

Overloaded and distracted to the limit. I'm at the supermarket on a Saturday with my one-year-old son, Nick, rolling down the fruit and vegetable aisle with a cart, thinking about how I also need to stop and buy dog food, fill up the gas tank, and pick up my truck from the mechanic's before they close for the rest of the weekend.

As I'm trying to prevent Nick from pulling the apples off the shelf, my wife Carmen calls me on my cell phone to let me know we need more milk and baby food, and would I mind stopping at the pharmacy to pick up the photos she brought in to be developed on Friday?

Well, while grabbing Nick with one hand and twisting my head to hold the tiny phone against my neck, I reach into my pocket with the other hand to take out my shopping list and a pen. Panic sets in.

I realize my cell phone isn't in there where I left it, and I have no idea where it could be.

I tell Carmen I can't find my phone. I think it's lost. It might be in the car, but I can remember taking it with me into the store and maybe it dropped into the bin of breakfast meats when I leaned over to pick up those boxes of bacon.

Her brief silence was followed by the obvious question, "Aren't you talking to me on your phone?"

More silence.

"Oh, yeah, you have a point."

There's nothing like working on your to-do list while handling a baby and talking on the phone in the middle of a grocery store to get you so distracted that you forget what you have right in your hands. At least none of the apples fell on the ground.

Joan Houlihan:

Delivering a baby is stressful business for everyone involved, especially for my husband Peter when he was about to become a father.

I delivered the first of my five children two weeks late. When we arrived at the hospital, with my contractions fifteen to twenty minutes apart, the nurse at the reception desk asked my husband for his first name. He looked her straight in the face and very calmly replied, "Paul."

Peter was twenty-five years old at the time. Do you think stress had something to do with it?

Adam Rosenbaum:

Going to the cash machine had become a habitual non-thinking action for me.

For years, every Friday night I went to the bank to take money out of the ATM, until one Friday I was in a hurry and couldn't remember the PIN I had used every week—for years! The machine spit my card back at me three times, and I went home in a state of disbelief and no cash to boot.

Out of frustration, I drove back to the bank the next day with the idea that I would approach the cash machine with a cleared mind and just let my fingers hit the buttons without thinking about it. One, two, three, four, and bingo. The money slid out from the machine.

At that point I realized I had not said my PIN out loud in years. The muscles in my fingers had memorized the pattern of the numbers, but I had forgotten them.

It Doesn't Take Much

As you can see, it doesn't take much for the Memory Busters to turn anyone's brain into mush. And it doesn't matter if you're twenty-five or sixty-five, because most of us can't go to the hospital without experiencing some degree of stress, and few of us can suddenly become interested in a subject like connecting a VCR.

The key to an efficient memory is learning to manage these situations by recognizing how the Memory Busters gum up the memory process and outsmarting them before they have a chance to distract you and make you forget.

Let's begin the attack on the Memory Busters by explaining how information overload operates and show you how to outmaneuver this obstacle so you can begin to turn your mind into a model of efficiency.

5.

Information Overload

Too Much Information

Information overload is the Memory Buster of the new millennium. It occurs when you are bombarded by so much information your mind can't decide where to focus its attention and your Short-Term Memory isn't given the chance to apply meaning to anything.

This is why your high school teachers told you to prepare for a test by studying for thirty minutes every day instead of cramming for ten hours the night before the exam.

Just like the other Memory Busters, information overload has affected human memory ever since people learned to do two things at once, but the society-wide epidemic of this Memory Buster is a true modern-day phenomenon.

How Did This Happen?

In many ways we've become victims of our own technological success; the reason this Memory Buster is so prevalent is the excessive supply of gadgets and media that were designed to enhance our lives by providing us with more access to more information.

Yes, the Digital Revolution has improved our health and modernized communication, yet it's also drowning us in so much data that our memories don't function efficiently anymore.

Let's take a look at how digital innovations have altered our lives in ways only the writers of Star Trek could dream of.

Today, you can:

- Communicate with your friends and family at any hour of the day, no matter where you are on the planet, with e-mail, cell phones, and instant messaging.
- Sit on vacation in the middle of the Mojave Desert and watch a live broadcast of a volleyball game in Brazil by pointing a portable satellite dish into outer space from the roof of your RV.
- Listen to hundreds of radio stations from around the world over the Internet with the click of a button and a few pieces of relatively inexpensive equipment.
- Get cash out of your US bank account from an ATM in Istanbul and check your stock quotes from a cyber café in Buenos Aires.
- Get a medical exam from a doctor who's in a virtual office two hundred miles away.

The list of information available to you at a moment's notice seems limitless. But think about this for a second.

How efficient is your memory when you're watching a cable television news screen filled with stock quotes flying across the bottom, the time of day in one corner, the weather in the other, and the anchorman telling you about taxes for married couples with 2.6 children one second and a bomb that went off in the former Soviet Republic of Phleblechistan the next?

Can you really focus your attention on the newscast, or does it all come at you so quickly that the second story begins before the first one seems to end, leaving no time for your Short-Term Memory to apply meaning, or chunk any of the information?

The Brain Strain

Do you remember any of it, or do all the flashing numbers and hyped-up sound effects stress and strain your brain beyond reasonable human limitations?

In our research into Memorology, we've discovered that even though it's nice to know you can reach people when you need to, and this may reduce stress (another Memory Buster we'll address later), the human race has survived for centuries without cell phones that have cameras on them and without the technology to beep your daughter to remind her to call you the minute her plane lands in Denver.

It makes you wonder how mothers ever sent their kids to the store without feeling helpless because they couldn't call to tell them to pick up two bags of shredded cheese instead of just one.

How did we manage without all of this new-age stuff? Our guess is that since our heads weren't so cluttered up with excessive information and we weren't distracted by so many beeps and buzzes, we were able to plan and remember much better than we do today. Currently, there is so much information we can't even remember a second bag of shredded cheese!

How many codes, PINs, and gizmos do you rely on today that didn't exist thirty years ago? Take a look at how many numbers and passwords Adam and Joan may use on any given day between 9:00 AM and lunch. And remember, this is just the tip of the iceberg.

- Code to turn on personal cell phone
- Phone number to access cell phone voicemail
- Password to enter cell phone voicemail
- Number to access work phone voicemail
- Password to retrieve messages from work phone voicemail
- Spouse's cell phone
- Spouse's work phone
- Code to activate home answering machine for remote message playback
- PIN for bank card
- Password to log onto work computer
- Passwords to enter programs on work computer you can only access after you log onto work computer
- Password to company travel reservation service on work computer
- Password to home Internet account
- Password to Internet e-mail account

- Password to online bank account
- Code for burglar alarm

Now add all of this to a list of responsibilities—job, appointments, carpools, schedules, kids, pets, parents—and you can see how it can become difficult to focus your attention on anything.

Beating Information Overload

Fortunately, you can get a step ahead of the information overload, and it's easier than you think. Do you remember when we asked you to look at a random list of words for fifteen seconds, and you remembered about six or seven of them? Then we showed you the same group of words organized into meaningful categories and you discovered it was easier to remember information that was chunked together?

The trick to preventing information overload is no different; it's as simple as chunking your information and activities in a way that forces you to remember not to forget. This won't require much effort because there's nothing to memorize here. Chunking your life together is as effortless as

- Cleaning up your clutter.
- Always leaving your things in the same place.
- Organizing your calendar with a set of color-coded pens.
- Creating acronyms and phrases.

Let's start with all that clutter.

Overloaded with Clutter

Reducing clutter is critical to an efficient memory, because eliminating a mess reduces randomness, and reducing randomness helps you chunk your thoughts and activities so your memory can use its storage space efficiently.

Could you imagine going to a library that wasn't cataloged into a logical system? You'd never be able to find anything. When your office is in disarray, when you have papers all over the house, and when some of your bills are in the kitchen and others are on the stairs under a pile of coats, you don't have a meaningful or systematic way of keeping track of anything. Your memory is inefficient because its only point of reference is chaos.

It's time to get organized!

Start by cleaning up your desk. Make it an efficient workspace, designated just for work. This is where you'll keep all of your receipts, calendars, Post-its, phone numbers, addresses, an inbox, and an outbox. This is your library of personal items. When you remove something, put it back in its place when you're done with it.

File important documents immediately in a file cabinet that happens to be right next to your recently organized desk. No more papers, notices, and tax refunds piled up randomly on the kitchen counter or under the coats.

Don't let bills sit around. Whenever one comes in, write out the check, stick it in the return envelope, and print the date the bill needs to be sent in the upper right-hand corner where you put the stamp. Then place the sealed envelope in your outbox and check it regularly.

Clean out the medicine cabinet. Get rid of the aspirin that expired last year and that container of goop that's been there so long you'd need a vice to remove the cap. If you have a bottle with three drops in the bottom and don't know what it's used for, throw it out.

Clean out the refrigerator. Get rid of the moldy green cheese and the milk carton that expired six month ago. (You can take a whiff of the milk if you like. It probably won't affect your memory one way or the other.)

It's an excellent start, and now when you look around you won't see chaos. In the next step, you'll begin to manage your loads of belongings that seem to get lost and forgotten just at the moment when you really need them.

Overloaded with Stuff

Let's loosely define "stuff" as all of those things you carry around with you: wallets, watches, purses, coats, hats, umbrellas, phones, beepers, keys, etc. You take them everywhere, but where do they go when you walk in the door?

Have you ever spent a half-hour turning your house upside-down looking for your glasses before you remember that you left them under your gloves on the top of the bathroom sink?

Is that where they really belong?

Just like clutter, random storage of your stuff breeds forgetfulness. The secret to overcoming the overload is to always put your things in the same place. Then you'll remember where you left them.

Here's an example: When Adam leaves for work, he takes a wallet, reading glasses, sunglasses, car keys, house keys, a cell phone, and a work badge. This is too much stuff to collect early in the morning as he rushes out the door, so all of the items go into his night table drawer the minute he gets home. When it's time to go, he opens up the drawer, pulls out the stuff and leaves without forgetting a thing. It's a very efficient system.

If you don't want to use a drawer, put your stuff in a large Tupperware container in the refrigerator, or do what Joan does and put everything you need for the morning into a basket by the front door. It's not important where you leave your things as long as they're always in the same place.

Once you get into the habit, you'll see that it becomes difficult to forget, because by reducing the randomness, you eliminate the overload. Not only will you remember where you leave your things, but you'll also begin to work with simple systems that help your brain chunk important details into categories. This skill will also help with the next topic: appointment overload.

Overloaded with Appointments

We all have tons of appointments, but most of us don't have a budget for an expensive personal secretary who can keep track of them for us. So what do we do?

Raise your hand if you have a day planner that's bulging at the seams or a calendar marked up in gray pencil and dark blue ink hanging next to a jumbled bulletin board on the wall in your kitchen. Hmmm.

It's not the greatest way to keep track of where you need to be. Here's a new system that will solve your scheduling woes, and all you're going to need are two calendars and a set of fine-tipped, color magic markers to make it work; one calendar will be a big, flat, desk-sized one with large blocks, and the other a day planner in book form. (You won't have any trouble reading the big calendar since you recently cleaned up your desk.)

Starting with your next appointment, take the magic markers and create a simple color-coding system for all of the entries on your calendar.

- Red for "must do" and "cannot miss" like a doctor's appointment.
- Yellow for birthdays and anniversaries.
- Green for fun appointments, like going to the movies or a golf game.
- Blue for regularly scheduled dates, like a weekly carpool.
- Orange for special events like the Bernstein Bar Mitzvah.

Applying this simple system touches all steps of the memory process by catching your attention with colors (sensory) that have meaning (short-term), which you have developed into a logical (chunking) and rehearsed routine.

Finally, write each appointment down in color on your desk calendar and in your day planner, and check them every morning. No exceptions! This extra step will ensure that you remember your schedule efficiently by rehearsing and applying meaning to every appointment.

All right. You're organized and clutter-free, you remember where you left your colored markers, and you're on time for where you've got to be. Now, let's see how acronyms and phrases can pull you out of an overloading situation that's overflowing with information you need to remember immediately.

Acronyms and Phrases for Data Overload

If you're suddenly overloaded with new and complicated information you want to commit to your Long-Term Memory, create simple acronyms and phrases.

You've been using these devices since the first grade when you memorized the names of the Great Lakes with the HOMES acronym. Remember? Huron, Ontario, Michigan, Erie, and Superior. If you're in a tight spot and the words or numbers you want to memorize have no inherent meaning, change the information around and develop a quick and meaningful phrase or acronym for yourself.

Here's an example of how the US Marines have put this idea into practice. When Adam was in basic training, one of the first things the platoon needed to learn was the USMC ranks and insignias. Among the most difficult exercises was remembering the difference between the one, two, three, and four-star generals, and if you were quizzed on the ranks and didn't have the right answer, you would end up doing a lot of pushups.

To make memorization a little bit easier, the Marines developed the quick and easy phase: "Be My Little General."

☆	Be	Brigadier
☆ ☆	My	Major
☆ ☆ ☆	Little	Lieutenant
☆ ☆ ☆ ☆	General	General

This simple expression accompanied by a lot of repetition made the generals' stars unforgettable.

You Did It

In this chapter you've seen how simple it is to handle the overload of information in your life. You did this by

- Reducing randomness by organizing your clutter
- Developing meaningful systems to keep track of belongings and appointments
- Chunking new information with acronyms and phrases

At this point, you're beginning to learn that the Memory Busters are a force you can reckon with. Now that you've knocked the first one out of the ballpark, let's move on to Memory Buster number two: inattention.

6.

Inattention

Could You Repeat That?

Inattention is the result of distractions, a lack of motivation, and a lack of confidence that prevents you from paying attention to activities and information. Young or old, there is nothing else that catches you off-guard so frequently.

- Simple distractions draw your attention away from your own actions, which is why you can set the remote control down and forget where you put it just a few seconds later.
- A lack of motivation is the reason why your kids can't "remember" to take out the garbage.
- A lack of confidence is what prevented Joan from paying attention to her son as he explained the steps to hook up a VCR.

This chapter won't provide you with a special magical formula that will inspire your children to remember to take out the trash, but it will teach you to make your memory more efficient by using your senses both to focus your attention on important information and to ignore the diversionary tactics of inattention. You'll see that this is an easy Memory Buster to beat when you begin to

- Talk to yourself out loud
- Get your "hands on" new activities and learn by doing
- Turn off the TV and the background noise
- Show interest in new things

Let's start with talking to yourself. And don't worry, men in white coats aren't going to come and take you away!

Talk to Yourself

Talking to yourself is the solution for simple distractions and absentmindedness. It works by increasing the amount of sensory information you expose yourself to and adds meaning to your ideas and actions. Here's an example.

You come rushing into the house and you're immediately bombarded by a barking dog, your daughter (who's heading out with five of her friends), a pile of laundry on the couch, and a mess of dishes in the sink. Amidst all of the commotion, you set your keys on top of the bookcase in the living room without ever realizing what you did, since you're usually in the habit of putting your stuff in its proper place.

Later, as you rush out the door to your next appointment, you realize you don't know where your keys are, and you spend the next fifteen minutes in a frenzied search before you find them sitting on top of the bookcase—right where you left them.

To avoid all of this trouble, the next time you're about to leave your keys in a place they don't belong, say to yourself out loud as you set them down,

"I'm putting my keys on top of the bookcase."

Later, when it hits you that your keys aren't where they're supposed to be, ask yourself:

"Where are my keys?"

You'll hear a little voice inside your head saying,

"I'm putting my keys on top of the bookcase."

And that's where you'll find them.

It's not weird science, just a powerful strategy that sets sensory information on a fast track to your Long-Term Memory. We'll bet that it works every time.

Get Your Hands on It

Let's keep going with Sensory Memory to see how your senses can be used to improve your memory's efficiency for more complicated activities, such as hooking up a VCR. This time we'll start with a question.

How did you learn to drive?

Did you learn in a classroom by memorizing which driver had the right-of-way in an intersection? Or did you learn in a Student Driver car as you tried to make your first left turn into a rush-hour traffic jam with people honking at you as you sat frozen and unable to remember who had the right-of-way?

Our guess is the more meaningful lesson was your experience on the road, with your hands on the wheel.

Now take the "hands on" approach and apply it to hooking up a VCR. Had Joan asked her son to explain the process while *she* connected the equipment, she would have been touching the cables and making the connections herself, learning by doing. Instead, she was only half-listening and half paying attention to the complicated explanation, and she didn't remember anything her son said.

Often, when someone shows you how to do something new and complicated, it's very difficult to devote your full attention to the demonstration, because in your mind you're thinking, "I am never going to remember this."

This lack of confidence tricks you into not paying attention and decreases the efficiency of your memory. To defeat this

Memory Buster, start to touch, taste, smell, and learn like a little kid by getting your hands onto everything.

This way you'll focus all of your attention, so the experience becomes meaningful. Whether you're learning to work with computers or cook a chicken, your senses will do the memory work for you.

Turn Off the Background Noise

Keep the focus on your senses, because now you're going to learn how background noise works like a hit man for inattention by wiping your memory's efficiency out.

Background noise is a fatal distraction that prevents you from chunking and organizing your thoughts and activities.

If you're trying to have an important conversation with someone while keeping one eye and one ear tuned to the evening news, which information breaks through the Sensory Memory filter? The sound and the movement from the television? Or the words in your conversation?

If you're studying for a history exam while watching Monday Night Football or listening to the smooth sounds of Frank Sinatra, what are the odds that you'll remember the year the Magna Carta was signed?

Since you can't pay complete attention to the conversation or the homework, each experience is significantly less meaningful and the details of what you want to remember will be forgotten. The solution is simple.

Turn the TV off. Turn the radio off. Turn the blender off. Turn the noise *off!*

When something is important and requires your complete attention, and possibly someone else's complete attention, get rid of the sensory interference to ensure that your effort is as meaningful and memorable as it can be.

Show an Interest in New Things

Finally, to truly combat the tactics of inattention, start to treat your brain like a muscle that needs to be taken to the gym on a regular basis.

Since your brain is attached to the rest of your body, the same rules apply to both. When your body doesn't get any exercise, it gets flabby, and when your brain isn't challenged, it turns into a couch potato that allows inattention to take over.

Any number of factors can contribute to your mind becoming inattentive, including

- Depression, which can be a major factor for people of any age. (We'll talk more about this Memory Buster later.)
- Spending all of your free time in front of the TV without ever reading a book or planting a tree. (It will turn you into a zombie.)
- Becoming so consumed by your job that you can't "leave it at the office."
- The tendency to repeat the same stories from the past.

Regardless of the reason why your mind has fallen out of form, when you fail to pay attention to the rest of the world you can become disinterested, and even develop a fear of new ideas, all of which leads to a victory for inattention. Again, the solution is simple.

Do a jigsaw puzzle. Take a computer class. Make a new quilt. Teach yourself to play chess. Take a scuba diving lesson. Go to Macy's and check out the new fashions. Go to Wal-Mart and check out the new tools. Go to the movies. Try Peruvian food. Read a book from a new author. (We recommend *How to Remember Not to Forget by Joan Who? and Adam Rosensomething.*) Take a trip to South Dakota. Turn on the Spanish channel and try to figure out what they're saying.

The idea is to try new things to flex your mind and remain aware of the information around you. This in turn keeps your confidence high and your memory conditioned, ready to remember whatever comes your way.

You Did It

In this chapter you've seen how easily simple distractions and a lack of confidence and motivation interfere with your ability to pay attention to important information. You learned how this attention deficit leads to an inefficient memory by causing new information to quickly lose its meaning.

You also discovered that you can prevent inattention by

- Talking to yourself
- Using your senses and learning by doing

- Turning off the background noise
- Keeping your brain exercised and in shape by exploring new ideas

Now that you know how to create a line of defense against information overload, as well as inattention, we're going to show you how to do the same with the next Memory Buster: mindless repetition.

7.

Mindless Repetition

Over and Over and Over Again

Mindless repetition refers to the activities you repeat so often that they lose their meaning because you don't pay attention to them anymore.

You've seen this Memory Buster at work when Adam forgot his PIN at the cash machine. Mindless repetition also struck Joan one unforgettable morning when she spent twenty minutes walking around a hotel parking lot in Louisville looking for her rental car by trying to activate the alarm on her keychain. After so many business trips, she couldn't even remember the color or model of her car, never mind where she parked it.

Have you ever been in a similar situation? Was your reaction the same as Adam's the day he woke up to go to work and couldn't remember how to tie his tie?

"I can't believe I've forgotten how to do this...I've done it a million times!"

If so, you've caught this Memory Buster red-handed and didn't even know it. When you repeat an action a million times over, mindless repetition can easily pop in for a visit for the last two hundred thousand times and drain the meaning out of everything you're doing.

This means if you suddenly find yourself forgetting how to tie your shoes, it's probably a sign that your brain has gotten into such a groove that it put itself on autopilot and left your memory standing out in the parking lot, kicking cans.

With mindless repetition in the driver's seat, the muscles in your fingers may remember how to do the walking, but your memory is too inefficient to get up and dance to the rhythm of the funky beat.

To cure a case of mindless repetition, you must prevent it from happening in the first place. You can do this by

- Using more of your senses more frequently
- Putting variation into your routines
- Sticking up Post-it® notes when you feel the mindlessness coming on

You will also see why mindless repetition makes it so difficult (or so you think) to remember names and faces. But let's get to you senses first.

More Senses Make a Lot of Sense

Tackling the most basic version of mindless repetition is a lot like wrestling with inattention; you need to recognize when this Memory Buster is creeping onto your turf and then call up the reinforcements from your senses. Is this starting to sound like a familiar theme?

Think about every phone number, password, PIN, combination lock, and account number you've memorized and use constantly. When was the last time you actually read, said, or heard one of them? Could you say your cash card number out loud right now if you had to, or would you need to type the numbers on the bank machine keypad first?

To resolve this conundrum and get out of the rut of decreased attention, start to look at what you're doing.

The next time you call your mother in Des Moines or type the password for your e-mail account, focus your eyes on the numbers and keys and observe what your hands are up to. Don't just let them push and dial while your memory goes on a vacation to the Bahamas.

Also, say the numbers and letters, either in your head or with your voice. If you're not in a place where you can repeat the numbers out loud, say them to yourself in your mind. Otherwise, out loud is best because it maximizes the use of your senses.

By looking, seeing, listening, and thinking about what you're doing, mindless repetition won't be able to sneak up on you. And we'll keep repeating it—the more you use your senses, the more efficiently you'll be able to remember.

Just keep in mind that your senses won't volunteer for overtime, so you're the one who needs to keep them ready to jump into action.

Variation is the Spice of Life

In the previous chapter we discussed the benefits of exercising your brain and trying new things to keep your memory alert and attentive. For mindless repetition, you want to do something similar and stretch the areas of your memory that have become mechanical in order to refocus your attention on what you already know how to do.

It's no different than an athlete stretching his legs before a game or an opera singer practicing her scales before a concert. By keeping your memory warmed up, you will improve its efficiency and increase the chances of it being sharp when you need it.

To accomplish this, you'll need to change the way your brain is used to working by employing innovation and variation. Give these mind stretches a try.

- Take different streets on the way home from work or the store.
- Enter and exit your home, using different doors or sidewalks or paths.
- Get dressed with your eyes closed.
- Use your less dominant hand to
    - Brush your teeth
    - Comb your hair

> - Dial the phone
> - Put on makeup (Joan did this and ended up look-ing a little bit like Bozo. She had a good laugh.)

- Switch the side of the bed where you sleep with your spouse.
- Quit using the speed dial on your phone. Force yourself to dial the number and say it out loud when you do it.
- Make up a word for the numbers of your PIN or your brother's telephone number.

Can you still remember who you're going to call if you're in New York and you need a new mattress?

These stretches are simple. They immediately awaken your brain, both by pulling your memory out of its repetitive rut and by refocusing your attention.

Post It

While increasing sensory information and variation are excellent starts for combating mindless repetition, not all replication or duplication can be categorized into the universe of PINs and passwords. Actually, many repeated activities include errands such as picking up your shirts from the dry cleaner, and regularly-scheduled tasks like putting out the trash for the weekly collection.

The problem is that you often forget about completing these chores, in spite of the fact that you make mental notes to help yourself remember. Why?

Putting your garbage at the curbside and going to the dry cleaners are mindless events that aren't particularly meaningful. In fact, you probably remember to put the trash out only after seeing the neighbors' garbage cans at the edge of their driveways.

Since mental notes are no guarantee that you'll remember not to forget, we've come up with a simple solution: instead of a mental note, try a Post-it ® note! Buy them in all sizes and colors. A dozen pads cost just a few dollars, and they're perfect for the critical reminders you want to remember and cannot run the risk of forgetting.

Use Post-it ® notes in highly visible locations that are guaranteed to catch your attention:

- The bathroom mirror or the top of the toilet seat to remind yourself to put the garbage at the edge of the driveway first thing in the morning
- The exit door of your house as a reminder to take your shirts to the dry cleaner
- Your dashboard or steering wheel so you don't forget to mail your grandson's birthday gift while you're out shopping
- The refrigerator on Thanksgiving with a reminder that says, "Don't forget the cranberry sauce."

It's an effortless system, because the Post-it ® notes do all the work. Think about it. With the Post-it ® procedure in place you won't ever have to call your grandson in California to tell him that he'll be getting a big surprise the day *after* his birthday.

Remembering Names

It's a rare person who hasn't had trouble remembering names, primarily due to the mindless mechanics and stress involved in the meet-and-greet process.

You introduce yourself to someone and that person introduces himself to you. Then habitually, instead of focusing on the name for even a moment, you immediately begin to talk or think about something else. Within five seconds you can't remember the person's name to save your life.

That's when your husband pops into the conversation and you have to introduce everyone. Ouch!

It would be so easy if everyone would just wear nametags all the time or if you could stick Post-its on everyone's forehead. Since that's impossible, use this plan instead to help focus your attention and increase the meaning of new names and faces.

Whenever you meet someone, say their name out loud immediately after they introduce themselves. For example, Adam says to Joan, "Hi, I'm Adam." Joan replies back, "Hi, Adam, I'm Joan." Saying the name immediately and frequently keeps it fresh in your Short-Term Memory by taking advantage of your Sensory Memory.

Go to social events intending to leave with five new first names. If you keep this goal in mind, you'll find you pay more attention to people's names when they introduce themselves.

Try to associate each new name with something meaningful. For example, if someone's name is Joseph, link the name to St. Joseph's, the high school your brother attended or the famous musical *Joseph and the Technicolor Dreamcoat*. It doesn't matter if the name association is absurd, as long as it helps you remember not to forget.

Introduce yourself to others using a meaningful reminder. For example, Joan frequently introduces herself as "Joan Houlihan, like 'Hot Lips' from MASH." Create a clue for your name and use it when you meet new people. With a little luck, you'll have everyone introducing themselves with meaningful clues of their own.

Finally, if you see someone struggling with names, help them out. They may do the same for you.

You Did It

In this chapter you've seen how mindless repetition interferes with your memory, and you also discovered how to dramatically increase your odds of remembering PINs, passwords, phone numbers, and the cranberry sauce on Thanksgiving by

- Using more of your senses more frequently
- Putting variation into your routines
- Sticking up Post-it ® notes when you feel the mindlessness coming on

You also learned the skill of remembering new names and faces by focusing on two common themes in this book.

- Increasing your exposure to sensory information, which forces you to pay more attention to activities that are mindless and repetitive.
- Creating meaning around information to increase the chances of moving new names from Short-Term Memory to Long-Term Memory.

In addition to attention and meaning, another underlying premise of Memorology is that you have much more control over your memory than you ever believed.

This fact has become clear as you've seen the results of challenging information overload, inattention, and mindless repetition.

In the next chapter you're going to learn how you can control your memory's efficiency even more by focusing on your physical health and discovering how a healthy body promotes an efficient memory.

8.

Unhealthy Habits

Where Your Body Meets Your Brain

In your quest to improve the efficiency of your memory, you must understand how the health of your body is linked to the health of your brain.

With a healthy body, you feel engaged and you have an easier time paying attention to the information that surrounds you. On the other hand, with an unhealthy body you feel lethargic and disconnected, and shifting your attention into gear can be as tough as starting an old lawnmower that's been sitting in the garage all winter.

Fortunately, developing healthy habits to increase your brainpower won't involve an exotic new health plan requiring a special herbal concoction from the Amazon rainforest. As a matter of fact, the healthy habits we recommend are those you've been hearing about since you were three years old.

The difference is that you're going to discover why good health makes good sense for an efficient memory. You can do this by

- Eating a healthy and nutritious diet
- Taking vitamins and supplements
- Drinking plenty of water
- Exercising
- Reducing the odds of a silent stroke

After you read this chapter, make an appointment with your doctor to review your physical health. With any recommendation affecting your body, it is essential that you discuss and identify all risks with a medical professional.

Let's begin with the basics of the Memorology diet.

Stay Away From Junk Food

Everyone knows the phrase "you are what you eat," but what a lot of people don't realize is that food affects your brain as much as it affects the rest of your body. When you feed yourself junk, you're also feeding junk to your brain and can expect a poor performance.

To avoid a classic case of "garbage in, garbage out," start by staying away from the sugar and junk food. They have absolutely no memory value and are devoid of the nutrients your brain needs to operate efficiently.

To process sugar and junk food, your body consumes its resources of Vitamin B, which further deprives you of essential vitamins needed for healthy brain function.

Also, when you digest sugar and junk food, your pancreas puts the pedal to the metal and fills your body with insulin in order to lower your blood sugar levels. After your blood sugar rises and puts you on a fidgety high, the overload of insulin brings you down to a sleepy and inattentive low.

The presence of all this insulin makes you feel hungry and increases your cravings for more empty calories, which ultimately make you cranky and fat. A diet based largely on this Memory-Busting pattern of eating can lead to obesity, which is a major contributor to silent strokes.

How can you pay attention to anything when your body is being chemically altered like this? Just think of a group of seven-year-old kids, all wound up at a birthday party after eating ice cream cake and soda. They can't concentrate on anything for more than three seconds, and with a belly full of sugar and junk food, most adults can't either. What you end up with is hyperactivity, followed by sluggishness and an inefficient memory.

The Brain Food

So if a lunch consisting of a bag of pretzels and a can of cola puts your memory to sleep, what kind of food should you feed your brain? Our advice is the same whether you're a believer in a low-carbohydrate diet or if you prefer the Food Pyramid.

Ensure that what you eat includes the nutrients necessary to keep your brain and body healthy and running smoothly.

Fruits and Vegetables

The first step to a memory-efficient diet is to start consuming plenty of low-starch fruits and vegetables, especially dark-colored ones like blueberries, strawberries, broccoli, and spinach, which are full of antioxidants. (Antioxidants are powerful natural ingredients that protect the living cells in your body, including brain cells.)

Meat

For main dishes, make sure you mix your meats (lean red, chicken, pork), and don't forget about fish and eggs. They all contain high amounts of various vitamins and minerals, but the levels vary from dish to dish.

Bread and Snacks

If you're a bread eater, skip the doughnuts and the mushy white bread and go for the grains with gusto: whole wheat bread, low-carbohydrate multi-grain bread, oatmeal, bran muffins, and whole grain cereals—all are filled with fiber, vitamins, and antioxidants.

For snacks throughout the day, stick to things like nuts, in addition to fruits and vegetables. They're natural and nutritious, and they don't contain ingredients that cause cancer in lab rats. They'll also make you feel full so you won't have cravings for a bag of memory-numbing potato chips.

Dessert

Finally, keep your dessert portions smaller than your main dish. There's no sense in eating a nutritious meal followed by a gallon of ice cream. Eat a second piece of chicken or a bowl of strawberries instead. You'll feel better and think straighter this way.

Breakfast

One more important suggestion: do not skip breakfast. Your brain is a calorie-consuming machine, and while you're asleep it continues to churn away and work for you. When you wake up in the morning, your brain hasn't eaten in ten or twelve hours. It's hungry!

If you're looking for a specific diet plan, we strongly advise you to meet with your doctor or a dietician. But if you eat sensibly, keep an eye on the vitamins, and stay away from the sugar, you'll feel your memory's efficiency increase every day.

Vitamins and Supplements

In addition to the food you eat, talk with your doctor about how supplements like Vitamin B complex, Vitamin E, and fish oils can help your memory's health and efficiency.

The B Vitamins are truly the Brain vitamins. For example, a deficiency in Vitamin B-12 can lead to a range of memory problems, from the simple inability to concentrate to outright impaired thinking.

Vitamin E is an important antioxidant that protects brain cells and may delay the onset of Alzheimer's.

Fish oils containing Omega-3 fatty acids have a natural anti-inflammatory effect on the human body. They've been used to reduce high blood pressure, high triglycerides, stress, prostaglandin formation that regulates the dilation of blood vessels as well as improvement for a wide range of human inflammatory conditions.

Keep in mind this list of supplements is only a suggestion on where to start. Maybe a load of supplements isn't for you. Perhaps a simple multi-vitamin in addition to your healthy diet will contain everything you're looking for.

Explore and investigate. Discover what can help you keep your memory running on all cylinders, and then discuss an appropriate strategy with your physician.

Food Sources

The tables on the next three pages contain the United States Food and Drug Administration's recommended daily intake of vitamins and nutrients for adults (excluding pregnant or lactating women). We've also included some of the food sources for each vitamin and nutrient.

Nutrient	Recommended intake	Food Sources
Vitamin A	5000 IU	Milk, cheese, cream, eggs, liver, as well as green and yellow vegetables
Thiamine (B-1)	1.5 mg	Meats (especially pork), fish, peas, whole grains, and fortified breads
Riboflavin (B-2)	1.7 mg	Meats, eggs, legumes, nuts, green leafy vegetables, dairy products, as well as fortified breads and cereals
Niacin (B-3)	20 mg	Poultry, fish, lean meats, nuts, eggs, and dairy products
Vitamin B-6	2.0 mg	Meats, fish, beans, nuts, legumes, eggs, whole grains, and fortified breads and cereals
Vitamin B-12	6.0 mcg	Eggs, meat, poultry, shellfish, and milk products
Vitamin C	60 mg	Citrus fruits, strawberries, tomatoes, broccoli, potatoes, and cantaloupe

Nutrient	Recommended intake	Food Sources
Vitamin D	400 IU	The human body makes Vitamin D when exposed to sunlight. Food sources include fish, oysters, cheese, butter, cream, and fortified milk and cereals
Vitamin E	30 IU	Nuts and seeds, spinach, asparagus, seed oils, olives, and dark leafy green vegetables (especially spinach)
Folic acid	400 mcg	Dark leafy green vegetables
Vitamin K	80 mcg	Vitamin K is made by bacteria in the intestines. Food sources include spinach, cauliflower, soybeans, cereals, and other leafy greens
Biotin	0.3 mg	Eggs, liver, avocado, cauliflower
Pantothenic acid	10 mg	Eggs, chicken, liver, whole-grain cereals, broccoli, potatoes, and beef
Calcium	1000 mg	Milk, yogurt, cheese, cream, buttermilk, and dark leafy green vegetables (especially broccoli)

Nutrient	Recommended intake	Food Sources
Phosphorus	1000 mg	Meat and milk products
Iodine	150 mcg	Iodized salt and seafood
Iron	18 mg	Meat, liver, poultry, eggs, tuna, salmon, and dark leafy greens
Magnesium	400 mg	Dark leafy greens, soy flour, almonds, cashews, brown rice, and bananas
Copper	2.0 mg	Shellfish, whole grains, beans, nuts, potatoes, organ meats and dark leafy greens
Zinc	15 mg	Beef, pork, lamb, chicken peanuts, peanut butter, and legumes

Source: National Research Council's Diet and Health Report, 1989

Drink Plenty of Water

Water, water everywhere, and so much of it to drink, but many of us don't. How many times have you heard that your body is something like fifty to eighty percent H_2O? Did you know the percentage for the brain is even higher? As much as eighty-five percent water!

When you don't drink enough water, you feel tired and listless. This, in turn, affects your powers of concentration and your ability to pay attention, which causes your memory to become less efficient.

Make it a rule when you pass by a water fountain—take a sip. Bring a bottle of water to work. Try a refreshing glass of ice water at 2:30 in the afternoon instead of your third soda or fifth cup of coffee.

And speaking of soda and coffee, yes they are liquid, but they don't hydrate you well.

Generally, in moderation, there's nothing wrong with any of these beverages. Who can deny that coffee wakes you up in the morning and really jumpstarts your engine when you need it? Who doesn't like a glass of wine with dinner or a beer while watching a game? Just not all day every day.

Too much alcohol, besides getting you drunk, can actually dehydrate you. And too many cups of coffee or sodas, which are loaded up with caffeine, can make you kooky and send you to the bathroom every ten minutes.

Focus on water. It's cheap, it's healthy, it makes you feel good, and most importantly, it improves your memory's efficiency.

Physical Exercise

Okay Sports Fans. You're eating well, drinking water, and taking your vitamins. Now it's time to get yourself off the couch and start moving your muscles.

Remember how we said earlier that maintaining an efficient memory requires an occasional trip to the gym for your brain? Well, the same holds true for the rest of your body. To have a brain that's in good condition, your body needs to be physically fit as well.

We're not saying you need to turn yourself into Arnold Schwarzenegger to have an efficient memory, but take the lead from chess grandmaster Gary Kasparov, whose training regimen includes swimming, running, and lifting weights.

A chess player needs physical activity to keep his brain in shape, because aerobic exercise contributes to a healthy heart and open blood vessels. This ensures that his brain receives the oxygen and nutrients it needs to keep his neural connections strong and his brain running efficiently.

Whether you're going to play chess or just want to remember your anniversary, start running, jumping, walking, swimming, or riding a bike. Ask your doctor or a personal trainer at a gym for an exercise program that's going to help you feel good physically and keep your mind working efficiently.

Silent Strokes

Finally, we need to talk about a health threat that operates secretly and has the ability to create all sorts of problems for your memory: silent strokes.

Silent strokes (medically referred to as "TIAs" or transient ischemic attacks) occur in your brain and leave you with small bits of dead brain cells. Attacks usually last for just a few minutes, and the symptoms—such as numbness, slurred speech, and dizziness—disappear quickly and are gone completely within 24 hours.

Over a period of years, the cumulative effect of multiple silent strokes can lead to a plethora of health problems, including larger strokes and memory loss. When you think about it, if small areas of your brain are dead, then portions of your memory can't work. This is a victory for the Memory Busters. Fortunately, you can lower your risk of silent strokes if you

- Keep your blood pressure under control
- Keep your cholesterol low
- Keep your weight in check
- Treat diabetes
- Quit smoking

Modern medicine has many ways of helping you manage high blood pressure, cholesterol, weight, and diabetes. It's important to keep appointments with your physician so he can monitor these vital signs. (Keep your multi-colored pens handy and calendars up-to-date.)

Quitting smoking, on the other hand, is tougher than a trip to the doctor and a nicotine patch. But the addiction is beatable, and it's important that you kick this habit, since smoking not only raises your blood pressure, it also prevents oxygen from reaching your brain.

This will take willpower, but your efforts will go a long way toward helping you avoid a stroke—silent or otherwise. Remember that!

You Did It

In this chapter you've learned how being healthy, hydrated, and properly nourished helps you focus your attention and improve the efficiency of your memory. This is accomplished by

- Eating a healthy and nutritious diet
- Taking vitamins and supplements
- Drinking plenty of water
- Exercising
- Reducing the odds of a silent stroke

Are you feeling good about your memory yet? You're going to feel even better as you learn to take on the grizzly bear of the Memory Busters: stress.

9.

Stress

A Bear of a Memory Buster

Stress is the grizzly bear of the Memory Busters because it makes you feel like you're standing three feet away from a growling eight-hundred pound bear with big teeth who's looking directly at you.

Scientifically speaking, stress is the result of a complex communication system in your body that increases the level of hormones called "adrenaline" and "cortisol" when you sense danger. If you hear a noise in the middle of the night and think someone is breaking into your house, the combination of these hormones causes your

- Heart to race and your blood pressure to rise as more blood gets pumped to your muscles

- Pupils to dilate, enabling you to see more of your surroundings
- Attention to focus on the source of danger

In this situation, your body also shuts down non-essential functions to summon the energy needed to defend itself or escape. This reflex is known as the "fight or flight response" and has been an essential component of human survival since our caveman days.

Unfortunately, your brain doesn't differentiate between stress related to danger and stress from other sources, so whether you're looking down the barrel of a gun or just dealing with day-to-day tension and low-level stress, your body's cortisol levels will rise to some degree and divert your attention.

In the absence of any real danger, stress becomes a Memory Buster, and it's the reason why Joan's husband couldn't remember his own name at the hospital that day.

To identify and overcome the effects of stress, we're going to prescribe the following regimen to improve your memory's efficiency:

- Learn relaxation techniques
- Schedule time to worry
- Practice healthy habits (again)
- Get a good night's sleep

We'll start by showing you how relaxing can help you beat this Memory Buster.

Relax!

Moments of intense stress will make you feel like your blood is boiling and cause your memory to cancel its subscription to your brain. However, if you're not in any real danger, you can prevent stress from taking control of your memory by learning to relax.

The next time your seventeen-year-old daughter announces that she's going to marry her boyfriend who has five earrings in his face and plans to make a living as a professional snowboarder, try one of these relaxation techniques:

- Breathe deeply
- Picture a peaceful place
- Flex your muscles

Humans tend to take short, quick breaths in moments of high stress. To settle yourself, consciously take long, deep, controlled breaths. First, inhale slowly through your nose for seven seconds, then exhale through your nose for another seven seconds.

Repeat the process ten times as you focus on your breathing. Once you've inhaled and exhaled ten times, you'll feel more relaxed, the quick breathing should stop, you should be able to remember your own name, and you won't want to strangle your daughter.

While you're doing the breathing exercise, think of a peaceful place with blue water and blue skies, like Lake Tahoe or Cap Cod. Focus on the cool colors and fresh air and feel the stress begin to leave your body as the levels of cortisol in your bloodstream decrease while your daughter's fiancé fades from your thoughts.

Muscle exercises are another good technique for reducing stress, since they metabolize some of the hormones that force the fight or flight response and divert your attention away from the source of stress.

If the brief conversation with your daughter has you ready to fight, go to a quiet room, shut the door, and lie down on the floor without crossing your arms or your legs.

One-by-one, tense every muscle in your body for five seconds, then release. Do this exercise five times for your right foot, then five times for your left foot. Then do your calves, thighs, stomach, hands, arms, all the way up to your ears and forehead.

The entire routine shouldn't take more than ten minutes, but using all of that energy to work your muscles will help you relax and get your cortisol levels out of the stratosphere.

Schedule Time to Worry

Endless aggravation or worrying will cause prolonged low-level stress because the source of the problem, such as a bullying boss or a difficult relationship, rarely gets resolved. Since you can't fix the problem, you tend to tense up until you've worked yourself into a snit, which usually creates more stress and a less efficient memory.

Here's an example: Adam has a friend named Kevin, whose family was involved in an exhausting and grating lawsuit. The legal expenses were exorbitant, and for more than two years there was no end in sight. The stress was becoming so destructive that Kevin and his wife decided to see a psychologist to determine how they could improve their situation.

The psychologist made a simple recommendation: since they couldn't control the legal wrangling or slow pace of the process and since their day-to-day hand-wringing didn't make things any better, they should stop thinking about the legal case twenty-four hours a day and schedule a specific time to worry.

They did. And it helped. A lot.

If you're subjected to a situation like Kevin's, where you've exhausted all of your options and the only thing you can do is sit there and stew for hours on end, take out your color-coded calendar and schedule an hour or two when it's convenient to think about the problem or talk about it with someone else.

Once you know you've scheduled the time to stress out, you can focus your energy on more productive activities because you'll be under less stress, your cortisol levels will be down, and your memory will be working more efficiently.

Healthy Habits (Again)

You've seen how relaxation and scheduling time to worry can help reduce stress and improve your memory's efficiency, but none of these solutions will nail stress completely if you don't keep an eye on the healthy habits we discussed in the previous chapter. This is because the healthy habits that affect the efficiency of your memory also have a direct effect on your level of stress.

You already know that a balanced diet, plenty of water, and exercise are important for a healthy body. We also want to point out that a poor diet, alcohol abuse, smoking, and a sedentary lifestyle are major contributors to heart disease and sleeping disorders, which can impose severe stress on your body.

While many people try to relieve themselves of stress by drinking to excess, smoking, or eating gallons of ice cream, these behaviors actually increase stress, rather than reduce it. This can lead to a cycle of activities that causes more stress and results in an inefficient memory.

When you think of healthy habits, think memory, and also think about stress; this way you'll be battling the Memory Busters on multiple fronts.

Get a Good Night's Sleep

Sleep is absolutely critical for an efficient memory. If you don't get enough sleep, you feel like a zombie, your mental alertness decreases, and you increase your chances of experiencing stress, anxiety, and depression.

A number of factors contribute to problems with sleep, including

- Sleep disorders, such as insomnia, a chronic lack of sleep, and sleep apnea, in which breathing is interrupted during sleep
- Changes in mental and physical health
- Side effects from medications
- Excessive consumption of caffeine
- Smoking, which leads to nicotine withdrawal in the middle of the night
- Changes in lifestyle, such as heading off to college or suddenly becoming physically inactive

Age is also a contributing factor to sleep. As you get older, especially after age fifty, you tend to spend less time in the most restful stages of deep sleep. You also experience a decline in the night-time surge of the sleep hormone, melatonin.

If your memory is operating inefficiently and you recognize that you're not getting enough sleep, speak with your physician about the factors that may be contributing to your restless nights.

Also, consider taking supplements of melatonin, which are available over-the-counter in pill form. This may help you fall asleep more easily and can also help your body and your brain get back on track when you're suffering from jetlag.

You Did It

In this chapter you've seen how stress works on your body and how cortisol regulates the levels of this Memory Buster.

Most importantly, you've discovered methods to keep stress under control.

- Learning to relax
- Scheduling time to worry about your problems
- Practicing healthy habits
- Getting a good night's sleep

There's one more Memory Buster to go. Let's take a look at how depression will prevent you from remembering not to forget.

10.

Depression

Don't Bring Me Down

We've come to the mother of all Memory Busters: depression. It's an illness more people suffer from than the common cold, and it's not just a downer that leaves you feeling dismal and dejected. Depression also leads to

- A loss of interest in new and fun activities
- An inability to concentrate or pay attention
- Sleeping problems, fatigue, and sluggishness
- Eating and drinking disorders
- Stress, anxiety, moodiness, and anger

In other words, it's the Memory Buster that breeds other Memory Busters. And since the cumulative effect of multiple

Memory Busters contributes to depression, the problem tends to feed off the situation like sharks in chummed waters.

This means that if you notice you're having memory problems and you also find yourself not sleeping well, drinking too much, stressed, or overeating, you must consider depression. If you can stop this tidal wave, you'll cut down the effects of the other Memory Busters so quickly you'll wonder how you ever forgot to remember.

To deal effectively with depression and its effect on your memory's efficiency it's important to understand how your brain works when you're in good mental health and compare that to what happens when you're depressed.

Neurons and Synapses

Think of your brain as a super-computer made of billions of nerve cells that transmit messages throughout your body to control everything from movement and speech to ideas, emotions, and memory, but with one little difference.

Unlike a computer, which is connected with circuits and cables, the nerve cells, which are known as neurons, never touch each other. Instead, they communicate by passing chemical messengers called neurotransmitters through small spaces between themselves, known as "synapses."

This process is comparable to the transmission of electronic signals between cellular phones, which communicate without the use of wires. Here's how it works.

1. From a special terminal on the cell, neuron #1 releases neurotransmitters into a synapse.
2. These neurotransmitters travel through the synapse to a receptor on neuron #2.
3. When the neurotransmitters arrive, they generate an electrical pulse that travels to a terminal on neuron #2 and triggers the release of new neurotransmitters into another synapse.
4. These neurotransmitters travel to a receptor on neuron #3, and the cycle repeats itself until the message reaches its destination.

Pretty interesting, but what's really amazing is that the instant those original neurotransmitters from neuron #1 reach the receptor on neuron #2, they're removed and either

- Returned to neuron #1 in a process known as reuptake, or
- Broken down by a chemical called "Monoamine Oxidase"

In a depressed person, neurotransmitters are released normally from neuron #1, but when they reach the receptor on neuron #2, there's not enough voltage to generate that electrical impulse. Since reuptake or chemical breakdown removes the neurotransmitters so quickly, the message never reaches neuron #3.

This modest electrical malfunction is believed to be the mighty force behind the symptoms of depression and all of the trouble they cause.

Fortunately, there are electricians out there who can help you fix this malfunction. But don't look in the yellow pages under "E."

Treatment

If you think you recognize the warning signs of depression, make an appointment with your doctor to rule out other sources for your symptoms. Then together, you can figure out how to proceed.

Some doctors may feel more comfortable referring you to a psychiatrist rather than treating your depression themselves. However, it's quite common for a family physician to diagnose, treat, and monitor depression successfully. Generally, this is accomplished by identifying the specific symptoms of depression, and then

- Prescribing antidepressant medications or natural herbs that are appropriate for the symptoms
- Recommending psychotherapy to help you pinpoint and overcome the source of depression

Medication

Doctors use both prescription and herbal antidepressants to prevent reuptake or chemical breakdown of certain neurotransmitters and to improve the chances for electrical impulse generation. For example,

- A popular class of prescription antidepressants known as selective serotonin reuptake inhibitors (SSRIs) blocks the reuptake of serotonin, a neurotransmitter linked to depression.
- Monoamine Oxidase Inhibitors (MAOIs) block monoamine oxidase from chemically breaking down neurotransmitters. Both SSRIs and MAOIs are known to produce side effects.
- The herb, St. Johns Wort, is an over-the-counter natural product that functions as a weaker version of the prescription antidepressants without the side effects. It is sometimes used in cases of mild depression.

Psychotherapy

While medication and herbs have proven effective in reducing the symptoms of depression, medicine alone may not always solve the problem.

In addition to medicinal therapy, your doctor might also recommend psychotherapy to help you discover the underlying cause of your electrical malfunction.

Psychotherapy, administered by a qualified psychiatrist or psychologist in conjunction with medication, can be a very effective way to treat depression and improve the flow of electricity in your brain. You may be amazed at what you uncover in your mind, and it will also help get your memory working efficiently again.

You Did It

In this chapter you've discovered that depression is a Memory Buster maker. You also learned how a small electrical malfunction in the brain associated with depression can be treated with antidepressants and how medication can often be more effective when combined with psychotherapy.

You now have the skills to take all of the Memory Busters head on.

- Information overload
- Inattention
- Mindless repetition
- Unhealthy habits
- Stress
- Depression

This is an important accomplishment. However, even though you recognize the Memory Busters as the most common cause of an inefficient memory, sometimes doubts continue to linger, and there's still that one question on everyone's mind:

How do I know if I have Alzheimer's?

In the final chapter, you will find out what symptoms begin to surface during the early stages of Alzheimer's disease, how these symptoms differ from the effects of the Memory Busters, and what you can do if you think Alzheimer's is becoming a reality for you or somebody in your family.

11.

How Do I Know if it's Alzheimer's?

Don't Panic

You're having one of those days when you forget to pick up your wife at the doctor's office, then go to the company Christmas party and repeatedly call your boss's girlfriend Ophelia even though her name is Carol. Your wife wants to know who Ophelia is. You don't know anybody named Ophelia, and you can't remember the way to San José, even though you have a lot of friends there.

It's become quite obvious to you that Alzheimer's has set in and that you're about five years away from a nursing home, where you'll spend the rest of your life staring at a wall, thinking it's 1953.

This is not Alzheimer's.

Chances are you're overloaded, burnt out, and suffering from at least three of the six Memory Busters, so don't panic.

It's easy to understand why you might worry about Alzheimer's when you're really just battling the Memory Busters. According to the Alzheimer's Association based in Chicago,

- More than four million people in the United States have Alzheimer's disease, including ten percent of the people over the age of sixty-five and fifty percent of the people over eighty-five.
- One in ten Americans has a family member with the disease.
- One in three Americans knows someone with the disease.

In addition, there is no known cure for Alzheimer's, and the burden on family members and finances can be devastating.

It sounds like a lot of bad news, but before the cortisol kicks in, let's take a look at the facts so you understand exactly how the disease works. This way you'll see why a little bit of forgetfulness shouldn't spark fears of impending doom. We'll begin with the gremlins that cause Alzheimer's: plaques and tangles.

Plaques and Tangles

Memory problems and dementia have plagued humans throughout history, but it wasn't until 1906 that a German doctor named Alois Alzheimer discovered the source of the disease that bears his name: the development of plaques and tangles.

Plaques are sticky balls of gunk that accumulate in the synapses between the neurons and interfere with the flow of neurotransmitters. They develop when normally-occurring protein fragments aren't broken down and eliminated from the brain as they should be.

Tangles are fibers found inside the neurons that squeeze the nucleus. They develop when a protein mutation causes the collapse of microtubules, the structures that facilitate the movement of nutrients through the neurons.

The progression of the disease is categorized into three overlapping stages: early, middle, and late.

- Early stage: plaques and tangles develop in areas of the brain responsible for Short-Term Memory and the ability to carry out routine activities.
- Middle stage: Alzheimer's leads to the death of neurons in parts of the brain linked to Long-Term Memory, language, judgment, and behavior.
- Late stage: patients lose their ability to communicate, as well as physical functions such as bowel and bladder control.

Unfortunately for the millions of sufferers, no one has yet discovered why plaques and tangles develop or what you can do to prevent them, nor can anyone predict the length of each stage, since this varies from person to person.

And here's another curveball; no medical test exists that can diagnose Alzheimer's in a living person with one-hundred percent assurance since plaques and tangles can only be confirmed by an autopsy.

For this reason, doctors diagnose the disease by analyzing symptoms and then running a series of tests to rule out other causes. If the diagnosis is confirmed, a physician will prescribe treatments and therapies to help alleviate the symptoms.

The Warning Signs

The first symptom that usually comes to mind when considering Alzheimer's is forgetfulness, but forgetfulness alone does not mean that someone has the disease. The Alzheimer's Association has compiled a list entitled "10 Warning Signs of Alzheimer's Disease" that you should consider if you or someone close to you appears to be having trouble with memory.

(Reprinted with the permission of the Alzheimer's Association.)

1. Memory loss. One of the most common early signs of dementia is forgetting recently learned information. While it's normal to forget appointments, names or telephone numbers, those with dementia will forget such things more often and not remember them later.
2. Difficulty performing familiar tasks. People with dementia often find it hard to complete everyday tasks that are so familiar we usually do not think about how to do them. A person with Alzheimer's may not know the steps for preparing a meal, using a household appliance, or participating in a lifelong hobby.

3. Problems with language. Everyone has trouble finding the right word sometimes, but a person with Alzheimer's often forgets simple words or substitutes unusual words, making his or her speech or writing hard to understand. If a person with Alzheimer's is unable to find his or her toothbrush, for example, the individual may ask for "that thing for my mouth."

4. Disorientation to time and place. It's normal to forget the day of the week or where you're going. But people with Alzheimer's disease can become lost on their own street. They may forget where they are and how they got there, and may not know how to get back home.

5. Poor or decreased judgment. No one has perfect judgment all of the time. Those with Alzheimer's may dress without regard to the weather, wearing several shirts on a warm day or very little clothing in cold weather. Those with dementia often show poor judgment about money, giving away large sums to telemarketers or paying for home repairs or products they don't need.

6. Problems with abstract thinking. Balancing a checkbook is a task that can be challenging for some. But a person with Alzheimer's may forget what the numbers represent and what needs to be done with them.

7. Misplacing things. Anyone can temporarily misplace a wallet or key. A person with Alzheimer's disease may put things in unusual places, like an iron in the freezer or a wristwatch in the sugar bowl.

8. Changes in mood or behavior. Everyone can become sad or moody from time to time. Someone with

Alzheimer's disease can show rapid mood swings—from calm to tears to anger—for no apparent reason.

9. Changes in personality. Personalities ordinarily change somewhat with age. But a person with Alzheimer's can change dramatically, becoming extremely confused, suspicious, fearful, or dependent on a family member.

10. Loss of initiative. It's normal to tire of housework, business activities or social obligations at times. The person with Alzheimer's disease may become very passive, sitting in front of the television for hours, sleeping more than usual, or not wanting to do usual activities.

This list is not intended as a diagnostic tool, but if you recognize these warning signs, you should make an appointment with your physician and go prepared to describe the symptoms.

After a complete evaluation—which can include a physical exam, psychiatric assessment, consultation with a neurologist, brain scan, and laboratory tests—your doctor will be able to determine whether Alzheimer's is the likely cause of a patient's difficulty with memory or whether the problem is the result of another condition that mimics the symptoms of Alzheimer's.

What Else Could It Be?

A number of physical and emotional conditions can cause symptoms similar to Alzheimer's. Fortunately, statistics show that thirty to fifty percent of all patients referred to gerontologists for Alzheimer's are diagnosed with other problems that may be curable.

Four big ones are linked to the Memory Busters.

- Strokes: big or small, they can shut your brain down.
- Malnutrition: remember, you need those vitamins.
- Alcoholism: if you stop drinking, the symptoms may be reversible.
- Depression: unleashes the other Memory Busters.

There are also a number of other serious conditions we haven't talked about that can often be solved, but with more than just a healthy diet and exercise. For example,

- Brain injuries: even a light blow to the head of an elderly person can cause blood clots under the skin and put pressure on the brain.
- Brain tumors: they cause neurological malfunctions, but can be surgically removed in some cases.
- Medications: they always come with the risk of side effects. If taken in improper dosages, especially in elderly people, there can be consequences that affect the mind.
- Syphilis: this sexually-transmitted disease can affect your brain and your behavior.
- Endocrine and metabolic disorders: can cause dementia.
- Infections: can also cause symptoms of dementia.

The message is not to get discouraged and not to start worrying unnecessarily about Alzheimer's disease. If your memory is acting chronically peculiar, document the symptoms and then do what you would do for any other concern about your health and make an appointment with your doctor. That is how you'll get to the bottom of the problem.

What Else Can Be Done?

Sadly, the truth about Alzheimer's disease is that little can be done for patients except to alleviate the symptoms, and it doesn't matter how smart or successful you were in previous years. Authors, doctors, businessmen and former Presidents of the United States are all candidates for the disease.

Also, since Alzheimer's progresses slowly over many years, even family members may not notice the warning signs in the early stages. In so many cases, only when families have a diagnosis in hand and understand the range of symptoms do they look back and remember when the changes began.

On a personal or family level, the key to helping yourself or someone with Alzheimer's is to recognize the symptoms early and learn how to deal with them effectively. Denial is not an option.

On a larger societal level, research is the road to a cure. Scientists used to think that once a brain cell died, you were out of luck, but current research has revealed that new nerve cells can be produced even in a damaged brain. Every day we hear about medical advances for victims of strokes and spinal chord injuries, so we can be optimistic that one day there will be a solution.

In the meantime,

- Keep an eye on the Memory Busters.
- Be healthy.
- Watch out for the warning signs of Alzheimer's.

Most importantly, if your memory is operating inefficiently and you're feeling lost, pick up this book, go to your favorite chapter, and remind yourself how to remember not to forget!

12.

Resources to Beat the Memory Busters

You will find additional information about topics that affect memory, including Alzheimer's disease and health, from the organizations and internet resources listed below.

HowToRemember.com
Web: http://www.howtoremember.com

The official web site of *How to Remember Not to Forget by Joan Who? and Adam Rosensomething.* From here you can contact the authors with your comments about the book and success stories of memory improvement.

The Alzheimer's Association
225 N. Michigan Ave. Fl. 17
Chicago, IL 60601-7633

1-800-272-3900
Web: http://www.alz.org

The stated mission of this organization is "to eliminate Alzheimer's disease through the advancement of research and to enhance quality care and support for individuals, their families, and care partners."

Typical services available at local chapters include a telephone helpline, support groups, and education. Their web site includes information on risk factors, warning signs, diagnosis, treatments, stages, and statistics.

American Psychology Association (APA)
750 First Street, NE
Washington, DC 20002-4242
1-800-374-2721
Web: http://helping.apa.org

The APA is the largest professional association of psychologists in the world. Their web site provides information on a number of topics, including stress, depression, and sleep.

The Mayo Clinic
200 First St. S.W.
Rochester, MN 55905
1-507-284-2511
Web: http://www.mayoclinic.com

The Mayo Clinic is a charitable non-profit health organization, dedicated to clinical practice, education, and research. Their web site offers health information and self-improvement and disease management tools on a wide variety of health topics, including diabetes, heart disease, nutrition, and exercise.

The American Heart Association
American Heart Association National Center
7272 Greenville Avenue
Dallas, TX 75231
1-800-242-8721
Web: http://www.americanheart.org

The American Heart Association is a national voluntary health agency, focused on reducing disability and death from cardiovascular disease and stroke. Their web site contains information on these conditions, as well as recommendations on diet and nutrition.

The National Institutes of Health
Office of Dietary Supplements (ODS)
Suite 3B01
6100 Executive Boulevard
Bethesda, Maryland 20892-7571
1-301-435-2920
Web: http://ods.od.nih.gov

ODS conducts and coordinates scientific research within the National Institutes of Health relating to dietary supplements. Extensive information regarding the use and safety of supplements is available on their web site.

Smokefree.gov
Web: http://www.smokefree.gov

This web site, created by the Tobacco Control Research Branch of the National Cancer Institute, provides information designed to help you quit smoking.

Alcoholics Anonymous
AA General Service Office
Box 459
Grand Central Station
New York, NY 10163
Web: http://www.aa.org

Alcoholics Anonymous is a fellowship of men and women who meet together in order to stop drinking. The web site contains information on alcoholism and insightful advice that helps you determine whether you might have a problem with drinking.

0-595-32946-2

Printed in the United States
29155LVS00006B/283-303